Text
Miroslav Prstojević

Photos
Željko Puljić
for FAMA

Design
Nenad Dogan

Editors
Maja Razović and Aleksandra Wagner

Translation
Aleksandra Wagner with Ellen Elias-Bursać

The Guide to Sarajevo was written in Sarajevo between April of 1992 and April of 1993. This manuscript is part of a multifold project by FAMA, triggered during the siege of Sarajevo.

FAMA is an independent producer which in the prewar period anticipating the changes of the emerging postcommunism worked primarily in audio/video media, buying TV time on state television. FAMA has introduced a new genre for TV audiences - a political entertainment, which was a shock for a public used to the repressive tretment of politics as something deadly serious.

During the war, in the besieged city, under the fire of shells and snipers, in conditions impossible for life and work, FAMA began the conceptualisation of several projects with artists and intellectuals.

The Guide Book t"o Sarajevo intends to be a version of Michelin, taking visitors through the city and instructing them on how to survive without transportation, hotels, taxis, telephones, food, shops, heating, water, information, electricity. It is a chronicle, a guide for survival, a part of a future archive which shows the city of Sarajevo not as a victim, but as a place of experiment where wit can still archive victory over terror, the (sur)real "The Day After", contemporary SF, the scene of factual "Mad Max 5". This book was written at the site where one civilisation was dismantled in the course of intentional violence, and where another one had to be born, the one of 21st Century. It is the picture of civilisation that emerges out of cataclysm, which makes something out of nothing, gives some messages for the future. Not because the future is necessarily a future of wars and disasters, but because humans are growing older and being born into a world which is ever less secure.

SURVIVAL GUIDE

Contents

PICADO DE SARAJEVO

DESIGN ZULFIKARPAŠIĆ

Dart game

On the fifth of April, 1992, around Sarajevo, the capital of Bosnia and Herzegovina, which had about 500,000 inhabitants, around the city in the valley of the river Miljacka surrounded by mountains which made it the host of 1984 Winter Olympics, in the very center of what was Yugoslavia, appeared: two-hundred-sixty tanks, one-hundred-twenty mortars, and innumerable anti-aircraft cannons, sniper rifles and other small arms. All of that was entrenched around the city, facing it. At any moment, from any of these spots, any of these arms can hit any target in the city. And they did hit, indeed — civilian housin, museums, churches, mosques, hospitals, cemeteries, people on the streets. Everything became a target. All exits from the city, all points of entry, were blocked.

Climate

Sarajevo's climate is very continental, with a short hot summer, when nights are still cold due to the constant breeze coming from the surrounding mountains. Winters are rich with snow, from November until April. Snow had been recorded in August and in June — a fact which can be found in old Sarajevo chronicles. War so far hasn't changed the climate. The moon is still shining, the sun rises, rains fall, and it snows, too.

He has to have, and on a visible spot, at least one accreditation, seemingly just a piece of paper with his photograph. But beware — accreditation is the law in the besieged city, a proof of belonging to someone which makes you important. Those with local ID. are not more than the second-rate citizens. So, the modern Sarajevan has the accreditation, weapons, a good car, and a complete uniform. The owner of a bullet-proof vest is regarded with respect. The one who doesn't wear uniform, has an ax in his right hand for cutting down the trees, and a series of canisters on the left shoulder. His image would be complete with a mask against poison gas. A modern woman from Sarajevo cuts the wood, carries humanitarian aid, smaller canisters filled with water, does not visit a hair-dresser nor a cosmetician. She is slim, and runs fast. Girls regularly visit the places where humanitarian aid is being distributed. They know the best aid-packages according to their numbers. They get up early to get the water, visit cemeteries to collect some wood, and greet new young refugees. Many are wearing golden and silver lilies as earrings, as pins, on the necklaces.

Sarajevo is a city of slender people. Its citizens could be authors of the most up-dated diets. No one is fat any longer. The only thing you need is to have your city under the siege — there lies the secret of a great shape. Everybody is wearing their youthful clothes of teenage size. Sarajevans lost about four thousand tons (400,000 citizens lost about 10 kilos each). They greet each other with — TAKE CARE!

It is adapted to the potential sources of danger. Corridors and living rooms have been turned into wood-sheds. Hosts and visitors are sitting around the stove, feed it and stare into the fire. Everything is within the reach: books, tea cups, clothes, water, food. Everyone is ready to run into a staircase at the sound of a grenade, or into a basement, if there is one. In the basement everyone has a place, either the one that was fought for, or the one which had to be accepted. This space is ruled by the laws of community. Basements and staircases are special territories.

In the beginning of the war, a new social category emerged: owners of staircases. They established office hours. Those who are idle write down the name of each visitor, the ID number, hours of arrival and of departure — all very precisely, in a little book. A real spy book, in fact, like the proof needed by a jealous husband, or wife.

HABITATIONThose who were lucky, still live in their apartments. Refugees and those whose apartments have been burned or destroyed by grenades are inhabiting the apartments of those who left Sarajevo before or during the war. Temporary leases and bills of sale are being issued. Some entered flats by breaking the doors and changing locks. You can change the apartment if one of your friends manages to leave the town. Some people have two or three apartments. Depending on what each of them can offer electricity, gas, water, or minimal security — they move from one apartment to another. Those who are looking for you, will find you on the address where you collect humanitarian aid. Some are living in communes. Old families have disintegrated — new ones are being formed.

Windows are gone, destroyed by perpetual detonations. It was kind of pleasant during the summer — plastic came only with first rains. People were fixing it to the window-frames with wide tape used in factories for packing. Glue gave up under the rain and winds. Then people used nails. Whoever had no plastic — more than a precious item on the black market — would close the windows with cardboard boxes left behind from the humanitarian aid. The best for the purpose proved to be those smaller sacks for the rice provided by UNPROFOR — the only thing you needed was good friend who happens to be handling humanitarian aid!

Some windows are protected by the lumber brought from the basements and roofs. Those homes are dark as graves. Witty people are taking down doors from closets or rooms in order to 'fix' the windows and damaged parts of apartments. Bricks which can be found around destroyed buildings are used by those who still have walls and holes to fill. For the sake of security — merely psychological security — one closes windows with heavy cupboards, mattresses, books, carpets. Windows are dark after daylight is gone. People accumulate all their precious belongings in some corner of the apartment which they consider safest. Bathrooms, which somehow often happen to be in the center, are storage for paintings. Photographs, documents, jewelry, money, passports are in the bag next to the exit. In the bag are a few more items: medicine, zwieback, thermos, canned pate, and blankets.

Water

Water shortages may last for days, or weeks. The reasons are always the same — no electricity, or an act of terror. Then the search starts. First, one checks a basement. Then you may go to Konak (which serves only the privileged), then to Sedam brace on Bistrik, where big lines are formed, then in the neighborhood of Pionirska dolina, where one waits under the snipers. Those who carry water do so, depending on their strength and the number of canisters, several times a day, traveling several kilometers, waiting in a line for at least three hours. The lucky ones are those with bicycles, which are pushed rather than driven. The same with the owners of baby-carriages and former market carriages. Anything that rolls will do, for everything is easier than carrying the water by hand.

In one of Sarajevo neighborhoods, Alipasino polje, someone with a gun made holes in the water pipe running above a little stream. Water was pouring and for hours people were hanging on the rotten bridge trying to collect as much of a precious liquid as possible. The best thing that can happen is a discovery of water somewhere in the neighborhood where you live. It doesn't matter that the pipe emerges from the disaster left after the big Olympic hall has burned to ground. There is a pipe, and there is water, and there are big lines with people who do not worry anymore whether the water is clean, or not.

One of the ways to find water is using dowsing rods. Life, and your ability to survive is very much about natural talents. In this case — you put your electromagnetic waves against those of the water. Gifted magicians are searching for the water. Those more talented and skillful can even advise you how deep you should dig. It is known that even during the First World War, Austro-Hungarian troops had special divisions which consisted of dowsers whose duty was to search for new wells. At that time, the water on the Eastern Front (also known as the Serbian) was very polluted.

Yet, with them and without them, it is the rain that brings consolation. Groove gutters are, unfortunately, damaged. People stand in lines, in the rain, waiting with buckets for their portion of rain-water. Day or night — it doesn't really matter. People drink it and use it for doing laundry. It is very good for your hair, which becomes silky and shiny.Lack of water makes the people of Sarajevo very close to medieval knights and to French monarchs. They ration water, as if they were Bedouins. Long hair can be washed in a liter and half, the whole body in two or three — all in little pots and pans, with water lukewarm or cold.

The washing machine is a household appliance from some long-gone times. It has no function. The women of Sarajevo are again first-class laundresses. The only thing lacking is a battledore, lye soap and a clean river to wash what they have.

To run the toilet, waste water is collected, and water is brought from springs — if they are not too polluted — or from the street...

People of Sarajevo put daylight to maximum use. They go to sleep early in order not to use heating or electricity. They go to sleep early, because they don't see in the dark. They go to sleep early because the curfew starts at 10 p.m. and ends at 5 a.m. They wake up at any time during the night if there is a sign that water, or electricity, has come. These moments never last too long.

SARAJEVO BY NIGHT means that life follows the line of the sun. Without civilization based on inventions of two Americans — Tesla, who was born in the neighborhood and who we are proud of, and Edison, who they are proud of — you have to learn to go to sleep early and to wake up early. So many evenings are spent in envy of those who have electricity.

But Sarajevans have mastered the art of making kandilo, which is the light, usually hanging before an icon. To this Greeks have given the name — kandelos. Recipe: fill a glass jar, or a glass, half with water and a quarter with oil. Then cut five to seven millimeters of a cork, and drag through it cotton string, or a carpet fringe, or any piece of burning material. In order for the wick to stay above the oil and burn, a tin strip of some two centimeters is used and placed above the jar. Through that strip runs the wick soaked in oil.Candles have burned long ago, even decorative ones. People who have saved petroleum lamps are very rare, and for them a liter of petroleum costs 30 DM. Batteries ran out at the beginning of the war.

Light

Sarajevo by night

Still, they are being revived by cooking in salt water, five to ten minutes. They can come to life if connected to an automobile battery, if that one can be fed with electricity. All these tricks make batteries live five or six lives.

Of 1800 transformer stations in Sarajevo, more than half are out of use. To steal fuses is a regular thing. Three such fuses will cost you about 700 DM on the black market. Their real value is no more than 15 DM. Foreign currency is needed if you want to bring electricity from the station to the lobby of your house. To plug into a system, in all kinds of weird ways, is very fashionable. Another way is to run cables. You can steal the electricity from the houses which have it — on the right side of the street, and bring it to the houses which don't — on the left side. That has its price too, sometimes a deadly one. Some steal oil from the transformer stations to replace car fuel.

To have a car battery in the apartment, that is a real treat. A radio can be plugged into it — and turned on every hour, for the news. This battery is the source of light, too. Those less capable attach to it stronger bulbs and soon understand that the battery is drained too quickly. As time goes by, we all learned, and here is the advice — take the smallest bulb, like the one from the inside of a car. And carefully watch your lighter. You'll need it, if not for lighting a cigarette, then surely to climb the staircases.

Sleeping

Sleeping is entirely conditioned by the arrival of water and electricity. If they appear at the same time, the shock is complete. The race against time starts — in order to use both in the best possible way. It doesn't matter that it is two or five o'clock in the morning. We cook, we wash, we clean, we take baths. Sometime even a loaf of bread can be baked, the most wonderful gift.

Heating

Cold weather and the arrival of winter brought about new arrangements in the apartments. Chimney outlets were opened even in houses with central heating. From the basements and from the attics, from friends and acquaintances, old stoves were brought. Boiler-rooms are not working. In the absence of chimneys, people fix extra flues and stick them out of their windows. Flues are lurking on streets, smoking. Cooking still continues on the balconies, among empty flower-pots, housewives stirring the fire with newspapers. The basic stove is a tin one — furuna, made by craftsmen on Baščaršija or even by self-taught masters. Material and imagination define the form, size and the purpose (for coffee, cooking, or heating). Furuna are being sold on several markets, but only for DMs. But the major problem is fuel. You cannot buy wood or coal.

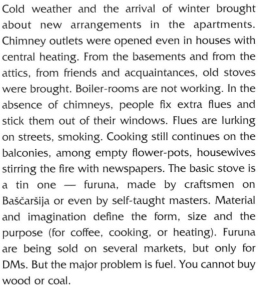

During the first summer, all dry benches, trees and wooden material were collected. This fall, parks, allees, courtyard and cemetery trees started to fall — birches, poplars, ash-trees, plane-trees, plum-trees, apple-trees, cherry-trees, pear-trees, all the way down to brushwood. Wooden backs of benches in parks were taken away, frames and doors of ruined apartments, handrails from the hallways, shelves from abandoned stores and kiosks, wooden stools and bars from restaurants, even the crosses and pyramids from the cemeteries. All bombed houses and barracks were dismantled with enviable speed. But fuel is still scarce. Those who were wise took scrap wood from their garages early in the summer. Now paper versions are being manufactured. Plastic bags, a part of US lunch packages — a leftover from the Persian Gulf War — can heat five liters of water...UNHCR supplied the city with a numerous but not sufficient thermal foils for windows. On every window, from the outside, one can read their name: UNHCR — they are the owners of our lives. November temperatures were very nice. Meteorologists have informed us they were very high, by comparison with times no one remembers any more: about 9 degrees C (Centigrade) in the apartment. It was warmer to take a walk then to sit inside. Fortunately, everyone can get warm while searching for water and wood.

The water from Sarajevo has always been famous. Today, it is being boiled and cleaned by pills. One pill for 1.5 liters! There is a white pill for two liters, and there is a green for five liters. Problems start when you have a green pill, and you don't have a pot big enough. The source of these pills is a secret which cannot be known. Pills are owned by the military, police, UNPROFOR, by the civil service...

Yet, the water, and tea, are the basic drinks in Sarajevo. The search for alcohol is long and expensive, as it is for the juices and milk. Parents are looking everywhere for the canned powdered milk — 35 DM per can, only. Peasants, who managed to save their cows and goats, are not bringing milk into the city. There are refugees in the outskirts of Sarajevo, who took their animals with them into the exile. There is a story about the woman who lives with her cow in an abandoned apartment, on the fourth floor: the woman inside, and the cow on the balcony. She is afraid to leave the cow for a single moment. According to some reports, another cow was seen in one of the villas of former revolutionaries, and in the neighborhood of General Morillon.

The main dishes of 1992 are macaroni and rice. You wouldn't believe in how many different ways they can be prepared! They can't be bought, except on the black market. That was the case during the first months of the siege. Now everyone is saving them, jealously, if they still have any. By additions and with a lot of imagination, one USA lunch package can feed five people. Rice, macaroni and bread are often eaten together — otherwise it is difficult to survive. For one resident of Sarajevo, during the first seven months of war, you couldn't count more than six packages of humanitarian aid. One had to invent ways to preserve and eat for as long as possible what is normally envisioned for one person, one meal, one use. In spring, summer and fall, all leaves it is possible to find were used as ingredients — from parks, gardens, fields and hills which were not dangerous to visit. Combined with rice, and well seasoned, everything becomes edible. Each person in Sarajevo is very close to an ideal macrobiotician, a real role-model for the health-conscious, diet-troubled West. A war cookbook emerged spontaneously, as a survival bestseller. Recipes spread throughout the city very quickly. People are healthy, in spite of everything, for no one eats animal fat anymore, nor meat, nor cheese — meals are made without eggs, without milk, onions, meat, vegetables. We eat a precious mix of wild imagination.

MEAT, if you have any, should be cut in very thin slices, salted, arranged in the bowl, pressed with some heavy object and covered by oil. Not the smallest piece should be in touch with air. That way it will be preserved longer, especially under your careful control. Better effects are gained if you fry the meat first, and then cover it with hot oil. You take out the portion planned for each meal. Another tip for preserving the fresh meat goes like this: wash it well, then roll in the napkin soaked in vinegar — that way it can stay fresh for a few days.

FRESH VEGETABLES, if you get it from someone's garden, or if you grow them in your flower pots which are by now cleansed of unuseful plants, or if you know of a park that's become a source of survival — vegetables like scallions, lettuce, spinach, cabbage, or anything that looks similar, should be cleaned, washed and rolled into a wet napkin. This is the way to preserve its freshness. Carrots and parsley should be cut, salted and packed tightly into jars. This is the way to keep them longer with most of their vitamins retained. You should squeeze all the juices from the vegetables like parsley and celery, and then dry them — that's the way our grandmothers did it many years ago.

Tips preserves

Cheese a la Olga Finci

4 demi-tasses of milk powder (bought at the black market)
1 demi-tasse of oil (from humanitarian aid)
1 demi-tasse of water (boil it first!)
0.5. demi-tasse of vinegar, or one lemon
1 small spoon of garlic powder (present given by a good friend)
Mix it all with a plastic spoon which can be found in the USA lunch package. The mix will thicken immediately, just like a pudding. If you were lucky enough to grab a bunch of expensive parsley, cut it finely, pepper it, and add into the mix. All should be then taken to your balcony, where the temperature is - 10 C; you can as well leave it in the kitchen, where it is only - 8. It should get hard. Even if you had other ideas, this dish has to be served cold. Enjoy!

A side dish - pommesfrites

1 cup of corn flour1 cup of white flour
1 spoon of bicarbonate (use the vinegar to neutralize)
Mix all the ingredients with lukewarm water. Make a dough, and cut it in the form of pommesfrites. Fry on hot oil.

Mayonnaise with no eggs

1 soup spoon of milk powder
4 spoons of flour
1 dcl of oil
0.5 dcl of water
1 small spoon of lemon juice
Mix milk, flour and water, and cook until it becomes thick. Let it cool, and then gradually add oil, and seasonings — if you can find them. Keep it in a cool piace, before serving.

Bean Pate

250 grams of beans
2 dcl of oilsalt, pepper, mustard, seasonings
Cook the beans and paste them. Slowly add oil and seasonings — as much as you like and have. Keep cold.

Pate ' 93 or Bread-crumbs Pate

200 gr. of bread-crumbs
some yeast
3 demi-tasse of oil
pepper, salt, onion, mustard
Sauté the onions until they are soft. Add bread-crumbs, yeast and seasonings, and cover everything with lukewarm water. Mix it well and leave on the cold spot before serving.

Brodetto, made of a canned mackerel, floating in the humanitarian aid.

Cut two onion heads and fry them. Add tomato paste from the can, salt, pepper, vinegar (or white wine), some rosemary and a bay leaf. When this is cooked, add a piece of mackerel from the can, and cook for five minutes more. As a side dish, cook porridge, polenta or, since you might lack all the ingredients, try some rice or macaroni.

Garden snails

After the rain, in the park or in the garden, find snails, wash them and cook as long as it takes them to leave their homes. Put them in cold water, extract the meat and cut it in tiny pieces. Fry two onions on some oil, add the salt, pepper, some canned tomato paste, a spoon of vinegar, a spoon of flour and two spoons of water. Cook well, add snail-meat, cook more. Try. Add whatever necessary. Serve with rice.

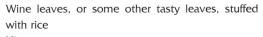

Wine leaves, or some other tasty leaves, stuffed with rice

History:

Once upon a time, this dish was made of beef, or of a mixture of beef and lamb, or beef and pork, with very little rice: this was stuffed in cabbage, wine or sour cabbage leaves.

Today:

30 leaves, young

10 dg of onion (or green parts of scallions)

rice, as much as you need, or havesalt, pepper, fresh or dried mint

Blanch the leaves, cut the onion and sauté it in oil. Add the rice, mix it with onion, and then add salt and seasonings. The mix should be placed on the end of the leaf. You should twist the side parts, and form a roll. Place the rolls in oily pot, cover with water and cook on a low fire.

Pie used to be one of the specialties of Bosnian cuisine. Woman's pride. It consists of a dough and of the filling. Depending on filling, there are about fifteen kinds of pies. Now it is difficult to speak of choice.

Dough

0,5 kg of flour
2 dcl of water
1 tea-spoon of salta
spoon of oil

Make a cone of flour, with a little hole on the top which should be filled with oil. While mixing slowly, add some lukewarm water. Mix it until it becomes elastic. Divide in three parts, and knead each of them with very little oil, until it turns into elastic ball. Leave the balls covered with clean linen on an oiled surface, for at least one hour. Then start stretching them, best using your hands, until you get the needed thickness of the dough. Should be thin as silk. Thicker ends should be cut, fried in hot oil—and eaten as snacks a la Bosniene.

Rice pie

Rice was never used in pies before. Now it substitutes for cheese.

Take 60 dg. of rice, for about three leaves of thinly rolled-out dough. Rice should be cooked with desiccated soup, or in salted and peppered water. It is recommended to fry rice a little bit, before cooking — that way it won't fall apart. Put the rice on the edge of the dough and roll it. It would be desirable to pour milk, sweet or sour, over the baked pie, but if you don't have the milk, water will do. Cover the pie, and let it soften.

Burek - Meat pie

Once upon a time, you would use fresh beef or lamb meat, cut into small pieces or ground; some liked it lean, some preferred it with fat. Today, look for meat in the cans from the humanitarian aid. You should grind it, add salt and pepper, and minced onion, if available. Dough should be divided into two pieces, oiled and filled with meat, then rolled. Arrange it following the shape of the baking pan — the traditional shape was round — sprinkle with some oil and bake in the oven. When pie is ready, sprinkle it with water, cover and let it soften. Serve warm.

Nettle pie

Cut the nettle leaves in the garden or in the park, wash it, mix with salt, pepper and corn flour. Cover the baking pan with dough and cover the dough with filling. Repeat, in layers, sprinkling each new layer of dough with a little oil. Put it in the heated oven. It would be great to add, once the pie is baked, some milk, or yogurt, or sour-cream. But lukewarm water will do, too, nowadays.

Sweets

Bread tart, a la Rajka

1 kilo of old, white bread
5 spoons of milk powder
3 spoons of cocoa
1 and half spoons of sugar
walnuts, hazelnuts, raisins, some rum, vanilla sugar
1 l of cold water

Cut the bread into small squares; mix other ingredients, cover them with water and let them boil. Then add the mix to the bread and mix it with a fork, or with a mixer, in case you have electricity. Pour it in a mold, and spread apple jelly on top and sides of it. The same can be done with pudding or chocolate. (Jelly is sometimes lurking in the aid package.)

Sweet zwieback, ekmek kadaif

In a shallow pan put mildly wet zwieback. In the meantime make sherbe (hot water with sugar, and some cloves), not too thick. Cover zwieback with powdered sugar, mixed with cinnamon, and top it with sherbe which should be added as long as zwieback doesn't take it all. Serve cold.

Easy Cake

2 cups of flour
1 cup of sugar
1 cup of oil 1 cup of water
3 soup spoons of cocoa
1 tea spoon of baking soda

Mix it all and bake. Top it with mix of one cup of sugar and one cup of water. Toss it with coconut flour, ground nuts — anything of the kind that you might find.

Halvah

1 cup of flour
1 cup of oil or butter
1 cup of sugar
2 cups of water
a bit of powdered sugar, or vanilla

Heat oil in a deep skillet until it boils, add flour and mix constantly, for it must not burn. Flour should get a caramel color. In the meantime, boil water with sugar and add this mix, sherbe, to the flour. Mix until halvah thickens, and then form small cakes with spoon. Toss with powdered sugar mixed with vanilla. Halvah is a very popular delight known since medieval times.

Or, everything tastes better than the boiled water. And, what are we going to do once all trees are gone?

Birch-juice

Young birch tree should be drilled. In the hole a few centimeters deep, one should install a tube. Leave it for forty-eight hours, while the juice is being collected in a tin. During April and May, one can get 8 liters of juice during 48 hours. Juice can be mixed with wine, sugar, yeast or lemon, and then left to ferment. This process demands several days.

Fir-tree-juice

Cut the needles of young fir-tree, and keep them in hot water for two or three minutes. Then cut them in tiny pieces, press, and put in cold water for two or three hours. If days are sunny, keep the jar in the sun. Filter and sweeten before serving. Pine-tree and juniper-tree can do just as well.

Boza

Once well known and very popular refreshment, gone out of style. Could be found only in two or three pastry-shops on Baščaršija.

0.5 kilos of corn flour

1 package of yeast

8 l of water

sugar and lemon-powder, if you have it and as you like it.

Put the corn flour in some water and leave it for 24 hours. Then cook it on a low heat about two hours, mixing occasionally and adding water. When it cools of, add the yeast and leave for 24 hours. Then add sugar and lemon-powder, leave it for three more hours and add 8 to 10 liters of water. Should be served cold.

Alcoholic beverages

Sarajevo cognac

3-4 spoons of sugar
water
ethyl alcohol

The quality of cognac depends on the brand of alcohol and on the quality of the Sarajevo water, preferably brought from some of the protected wells. Fry the sugar, add some water to melt it, and bring to a boil. Mix the water and alcohol in a ratio of 2.5:1, and add the sugar.

Wine

1/2 kilo of sugar
5 l of boiled water
1/2 kilo of rice
1 pack of yeast
10 cl of alcohol, or 20 cl of rum

Mix all the ingredients, and pour them in hermetically closed canister. Ten days later, extract the wine through a Melita coffee-filter.

Saki

5 l of water
0.5 kilos of rice
0.5 kilos of sugaryeast

Should sit for seven days and ferment. Then filter the drink and use rice in the pie.

News

The only papers you can buy during the siege are OSLOBODJENJE and VEČERNJE NOVINE. Once upon a time, OSLOBODJENJE had a format like the Times or Frankfurter Allgemeine. It had thirty-two, twenty-four or sixteen pages. Since June of 1991, its size started to diminish. Now it is of a mini-format, with eight or, more often, four pages. People who sell it are the journalists themselves — between 7:30 and 9:00 a.m. Due to the shortage of paper, editions came down to 10,000 copies. After November 1992, they came down to 5,000, which makes the time of distribution no longer then twenty minutes. Stronger readers seem to be winning. Radio Bosnia and Herzegovina, Studio Sarajevo, is broadcasting 24 hours a day. When there is electricity, one listens to more than just news. The news is broadcast every hour and everyone is waiting for it. Television today is no more than a few informative broadcasts, live programs and a press-conference held daily in the International Press Center.

Rumors

RUMORS are the most important source of information. They spread with incredible speed and often mean more than news transmitted through the official channels. They regularly — "this time for sure" — report on military intervention, on the siege of the city being lifted, on establishing corridors and safe havens. And they are regularly, each time "for sure," wrong. Rumors are spread by all: housewives, university professors, teenagers, doctors. No one is immune. They travel the City quicker then you will be able to, and they are mostly optimistic. Only later you might hear opinions that they were too optimistic.

The tradition of famous tobacco from Herzegovina and more than a century of the existence and production of the Sarajevo Tobacco Factory left a bad impact on Sarajevans. It spoiled them — people were used to the best cigarettes and tobacco for which special pipes, cigarette-cases and cigarette-holders were made.

Today, cigarettes are the biggest luxury and need. No one is quitting. You can buy them on the black market. Members of the army and of the police get them daily or weekly. There is no possibility of regular purchase. Matches too, are to be found only on the black market.

On some markets you can find tobacco dust, which before served as a high quality fertilizer for plants and vegetables. Today, that dust is precious and hard to find. Tobacco leaves are even more expensive and very rare.

The most passionate smokers are smoking tea. They are drying chamomile, Swiss chard, leaves, and cut it into 'tobacco'. That tobacco is then being rolled into regular paper or daily paper. Filters are made of toilet paper which comes as a part of lunch packages. It seems to be easier to find a pipe.

Tobacco

Not working since April, 1992. In the beginning, so called staircase-schools emerged where everyone gathered during the shelling. Now the education continues in the apartments, with children from different grades. Both high schools and grammar schools became homes for refugees. Classrooms and labs became dormitories and kitchens. There is laundry hanging on every school's window. Colleges work, exams are given, but only where danger isn't too great. Yet, many have managed to graduate. There is a lot of time to study. Computers and all the technology from the schools and from the colleges of the University has been stolen.

Schools

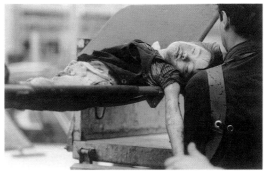

Stores have been broken into, shelled, deserted. This situation lasted for months and then, in October, a few brave owners reopened some of them. There you can find toothpaste, soap, toilet-paper (rarely), light-bulbs and foil for preserving food — remnants from the pre-war rich Sarajevo. Supermarkets are gone. Some, completely ravaged, since December are selling just the one and only kind of bread. People got food stamps sometime in June, but they never served their purpose — you could never buy anything with them. Only one card works, the one that appeared in December, for bread. If you manage to wait in a line, you can get 233 grams per person daily. Single men and women are forming trios, so that each of them gets a whole bread every third day. Business hours are from 8 a.m. to 3 p.m., but most places close at noon. At the end of a working day, merchandise is hidden in the basements, well protected and locked with seven locks.

Fashion

stores were selling until deep in the first Fall of the war: T-shirts, shorts and bathing suits. Winter coats were sold by smugglers on the markets where all of merchandise anyway comes from the deserted shops. Small sizes are the easiest to find, along with the luxurious wrapping paper and colorful strips for the gifts.

Drug-stores

are three, for the whole city. What they sell is simple and cheap, but when you buy it — becomes expensive, and rare. Tooth-pastes, shaving cream, cotton, combs and hair-brushes, two kinds of after-shave lotion, three kinds of bad deodorants, about ten colors of lipstick, one kind of skin cream. The same 'cosmetics' can be bought on the black market too, only there for Deutsche Marks.

Opticians

are selling about ten different frames for glasses, kept in the safe place under the counter. They don't cost too much. But people don't buy eyeglasses nowadays — they see all too clearly.

are two that are working, and one 'Book-Club' — Veselin Masleša — in which the number and selection of the books is rapidly diminishing. All the storefronts in the bookstores are gone, but no one has been stealing books. The storage of the biggest publishing house in Sarajevo, is now in the occupied territory. The destiny of those books is unknown. What can be seen is the growing interest for foreign-languages books, and dictionaries. Everybody seems to be interested in the languages of the world. Price does not matter

Bookstores

the most desired, are the shrapnel, which can be found everywhere: on the sidewalk, on the streets, balconies, apartments. Bullets are popular, but have a somewhat lower price. Some take with them food coupons. Other 'trophies' include war issues of OSLOBODJENJE, pedigree dogs, shoes made of snake-leather — excellent for running at crossroads.

Souvenirs

Gifts

for you will have friends to visit, should be useful. A bottle of clean water, a candle, a bar of soap, shampoo, some garlic or an onion. Passionate love is being expressed here by a handful of wood, a bucket of coal, a complete edition of books which lack humor and poetry. Could you spare some Vladimir Illich Lenin? Last winter has proven that his books burn well.

Abundance and color, choice and liveliness are gone from the markets of Sarajevo. There one can see poverty at its worst. Merchandise from all the tables can fit into two nylon bags. All the famous markets — Markale, Ciglane, Hepok, Alipašino polje — are now more like meeting points. Fruit and vegetables have been reduced to some scallions, nettles, cabbage, zucchini, small, rotting apples, green plums. All in small quantities, and all in DMs. During the fall you could find some pumpkins, potatoes from the humanitarian aid, nuts. The entire offer from any of the markets wasn't more than 20 kilos.

What you can also find on these markets are soaps, matches, lighters, pepper, cotton, old shoes, stolen wear on stolen hangers, salt, raw coffee. During November and December appeared cans from the humanitarian aid, home-made stoves — furune, nylon for window protection. Silverware and tableware, irons and axes, arrived too. Home-based manufactures released some of the most demanded products: marmalades, mayonnaise, cakes, pies, pastries...

Markets

Yugoslav money was in official circulation until April 1992. The same one, only with the seal of the People's Bank of Bosnia and Herzegovina functioned until December, for the country was without both paper and money. Since the new money for the Bosnian government printed in England cannot reach Sarajevo safely, bonds were printed in size of two tram tickets: 10, 20, 50, 100, 500, 1000, 5000 Dinars, all in different colors. The first four bank notes, when used alone, are worth nothing. The lowest prices are those of bread and newspapers.

One Deutsche Mark, which is the basic value for anything that is worth anything, officially counted for 550 Dinars of Bosnia and Herzegovina. At the same time, and on the black market, its value was 1200-1300 Dinars. The rest of the currency is measured against the DM, but is worth much less. The dollar is despised, and can barely be exchanged. Exchange functions only between the citizens of Sarajevo. Foreigners don't need to deal with it, for everything for them is paid. The biggest problem is how to change a bank note of 100 DM. You should have change — that you can use in the Holiday Inn, in the Bank of Bosnia and Herzegovina, and on the black market.

There is something new on the market of values. Papers: letters of guarantee, accreditation, military approval for leave of absence, a doctor's receipt that one is deadly ill, false documents of all kinds...Prices of these papers are between 100 and 300 DM, which is merely a matter of agreement. By now, the poor DM is quite inflated.

200 DM for 1 cubic meter of wood, but you have to pay 50 DM more for the delivery.

170 DM for a bottle of whiskey, or of French cognac.

120 DM for a kilo of garlic.

100 DM for a hare (white, weighing about 3 kilos), or 1 kilo of dried meat.

40 DM — for this you can get 10 packs of cigarettes, or 1 liter of oil, or 1 kilo of beans, or children's bicycle, or 1 can of fish and 1 can of pate, or 1 lunch package, or half a kilo of tobacco.

30 DM for a wool sweater (hand made) or 1 jar of fat.

20 DM for 1 kilo of onions, or 2 kilos of cabbage, or a big pumpkin.

10 DM is the price of four batteries of 1,5 V, or of 5 liters of water — at all times except the summer. Then the price of 5 liters of water raises to 30 DM.

3 DM for a chocolate bar, or a bunch of parsley. A circular saw is worth as much as seven kilos of onions. One liter of milk is between 2,5 and 5 DM, but can be gotten for a pack of cigarettes. This is the best exchange between babies and smokers known in history.

What functions best is bartering. For two kilos of raw coffee, you can get a propane gas bottle of 12 kilos. A package of antibiotics is worth two local phone-calls. For a liter of cooking oil you can get a carton of cigarettes and a liter of cheap liquor, or three liters of cherry-syrup. For two liters of oil you can wear almost new Reeboks. A used male winter jacket costs 3 kilos of onions. A once-standard package of 18 kilos of paint is being exchanged for any kind and amount of food. 10 liters of oil, the amount which supplies energy for the two-hour shooting of a TV broadcast about the future of Bosnia and Herzegovina, is exchanged for 12 cans which supply energy for your private survival.

In handwritten ads on Tito's street, one finds supply and demand ranging from gas stoves, jackets, shoes to messages such is this: "I am looking for a woman to help me survive the winter."

Provisions for winter

Firms emerged (Bankopromet, Generalmarket...) which offer food provisions for winter to shocked Sarajevans. One is supposed to pay in advance, in hard currency. Compared to the black market, prices were unbelievably low. After the first delivery, everything stopped. Suppliers were visited by some people who told them that their merchandise is far too cheap.

Sarajevo got its first park at the end of the last century. That was the Big Park, modeled by some governmental figure during the reign of the Austro-Hungarian Empire. Later, dozens of parks were planted with different trees and bushes, flowers and grass. They first suffered through the shelling, and then fell during the cold days and nights, cut by people who loved them but wanted to survive the winter. They did not believe anyone who reassured them that there would be electricity and that the heating systems would work. They were right.

The ZOO

which is located in the Valley of Pioneers (Pionirska dolina), is closed. The only inhabitants, still alive, are two ponies and several peacocks. Animals in the Zoo served as experimental targets for brave snipers on the nearby front-line. Others gradually died of hunger and thirst — their guards were too afraid to reach them. All perished — monkeys, llamas, camels, tigers, wolves, lions. The last died on November the third. It was a bear, whose innocent death was shown all over the world.

Wear and Footwear

Everyone is in sports clothes, for they are warmer, more comfortable and enable you to run quicker. Most of the members of the Bosnian Armed Forces wear deep white sneakers with the logo Yugosport. Their uniform, at the beginning, consisted of jeans, masking parts, ingenious improvisations made of bright colors. Bulletproof jackets are very rare. They can be found at the price of 200 DM. Citizens renew wear and footwear by moving into abandoned apartments.

Walking

Six kilometers a day—that is the average for those who don't need to go far. Some believe it helps you to keep in good shape.

Running

That is the favorite sport, practiced by everyone in Sarajevo. All cross-roads are run through as are all the dangerous neighborhoods. One runs with stolen wood, to the line where others are standing. Something is on sale, and you will know it only when you join the line.

Rock-climbing

Urban rock-climbing is a compulsory sports discipline. Instead of adequate ropes, one uses sheets. Climbers are solving distances between balconies, from higher to the lower ones which are not yet reached by fire.

Soccer

Often played with soldiers of UNPROFOR. On the other side — Bosnian Armed Forces, police and professional city players who are still here. Games take place in the hall of the burned Skenderija. The game is hard, masculine, with lots of injuries. Foreigners lose here, as they always did.

Chess

Played on staircases, in basements and in shelters. Sometimes even in the chess club Bosna, which has a good and very expensive buffet.

Tree-cutting

An entirely new city discipline. Tools for this sport are an electric saw and axes, small and big. One gets trained by cutting, trimming, splitting and piling the wood on the balcony or in the room, where they don't suffer so much humidity. Wood is stacked in the bedroom, hall, living room, in the next apartment whose owners have left or disappeared.

Cards
The basic mode of comradeship during the long winter nights. Takes place on staircases where it was the first possibility for frightened neighbors to finally meet each other. For those who know how to play and win, it becomes part of a survival-struggle. No one plays for money, but for a lunch packet, canned fish, liter of oil — that is serious capital!

Billiards
Banned in the nineteenth century, today it is the favorite time-killer for the jobless, school-less people. Some of them might become world champions.

Pinball machines
Work, despite the lack of electricity. Their owners learned how to solve that minor problem.

Children's games
Counting of grenades fired on the City, trimming fallen trees, collecting bullets, shells...Exchange of collections.

Speed
Dismantling the parts of abandoned cars and taking them away, into 'security'. Rule of the game: as quickly as possible. No age limits.

Ladies' talk
Exchange of war recipes: who can prepare better meal made of nothing!?

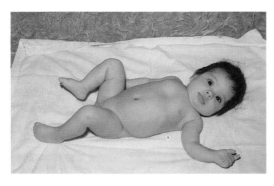

Transportation

Imagine driving through streets with no street lights (which are torn down or not working), without any traffic signs (for they are gone), without any attention paid to pedestrians, with a maximum speed across the crossroads and other dangerous spots. People are driving recklessly in both directions. No one pays any attention to crashes. Broken cars are being abandoned easily and damage is being negotiated in quick conversations. This is the war with the biggest civilian motor pool. The war is being waged in Audis, in BMWs, in Mercedes and VW Golfs, as well as in expensive yuppie jeeps.

The Sarajevo car of 1992 is a GOLF DIESEL. It is painted in military camouflage, and has no windows. It is entirely covered by nylon, foils, tin, cardboard and hardboard. Its fenders have been ruined, it is full of holes made by bullets, has no lights. Depending on the taste of a driver, or of his girlfriend, lights are covered with tapes in different colors: red, blue, green, all for a night drive in the city which is totally dark. Driving is fast and dangerous. There are no rent-a-car services. You rent a car with a driver — former taxi-driver — and you pay 100 DM per day.

City transportation — trams, buses, vans, trolleys, cable rail-way — does not exist. Sometimes, rarely, you can see double buses but only until October, almost half of a year after the war had started. A bus is running between Alipašino pole to the French Hospital (it was once military), in case it gets fuel from UNPROFOR. When the fuel is gone, passengers leave the bus and continue on foot.

Cars are running, if run by or for officials. Most were taken away form private owners, with or without a receipt, especially if they ran on diesel. New models appeared, home-made armored cars which look like moving closets, only with a hole in front of the driver. They are slow, shaky and loud.

Bicycles — which were never too popular in this hilly terrain — are being rediscovered and put to use.

Shopping carts are now used for the transportation of water canisters, of coal and wood. Renting is not too expensive.

Taxis do not exist.

Parking is advised only on spots protected from grenades and thieves. Such places are scarce. Whole cars are stolen, but their parts are not safe either: wheels, fuel, batteries, seat-covers, lights.

Gas stations are not working. Fuel can be found at UNPROFOR, and on the black market where the price per liter is 15 DM. You can get five liters of oil in exchange for a porno video — very appreciated by the Ukrainian members of the UN forces. Don't expect that the gas or petrol are going to be of good quality.

Car-repair, exclusively arranged through connections. There are no visible signs where repairmen are working. But they exist.

The main post office burned during the night between the second and third of May, 1992. What burned were the numbers of 50,000 subscribers, all which start with 2, 3 and 51. Later other numbers were disconnected as well, for security reasons. Since the end of July of 1992, Sarajevo has been completely disconnected from the world.

At the end of November, unemployed former postmen appeared in front of houses, bringing old telephone bills, and announcing the distribution of letters which might arrive through humanitarian organizations.

Letters should be given to the foreign journalists, officers of UNPROFOR, to the ministers who travel the world, or to the passengers of convoys. If letters are not confiscated at some of the enemy's barricades, they will go out of the city. People leave letters in the lobbies of different business buildings, at humanitarian organizations (Caritas), in the Adventist Church, with members of the Presidency of Bosnia and Herzegovina. For Belgrade and for the east of former Yugoslavia, all letters have to go first through Croatia, Slovenia and then to Europe in order to be received. An unknown man may meet you on the street, ask you whether you know someone, and if you do, give you a letter to forward it to the final address.

Letters

Very similar is the channel through which letters are reaching people divided by the division of the city itself. Letters may travel from one part of the city to another for more then forty-five days. For some areas communication functions only through the Red Cross. In order to solve the distance of few hundred meters, letters fly to Geneva.

City corespodence

Letters of Guarantee

Very special, and very much a war-phenomenon. Without them, you cannot leave Bosnia and Herzegovina, nor can you enter Croatia. No medical diagnosis will help you, no recommendation for an urgent hospital treatment. Not even the fact that you might be the owner of a house in Croatia. What you need is a letter from a citizen of Croatia which proves that someone is responsible for you while you are getting ready to leave for some other country. Otherwise, you might end in one of the refugee camps. Such a letter is needed for every convoy you might need to join, and the way it arrives is often quite magical: by mail to Split, then by a bus to Zenica or Kiseljak, then by fax to Sarajevo. Its journey lasts for days and yet, it is these letters that serve as the most powerful proof that the people of Sarajevo can deal with the impossible.

HAM-RADIO OPERATORS are a discovery for the people of Sarajevo. Only through their stubbornness can you get in contact with those you love. They are a connection between the East and the West. Conversations are short, and start with the punch line: "We are healthy and well. Over." All conversations and all messages are public. The room in which operators sit has at least five people at any moment, and the place where messages are being received has at least as many. Intimacy is gone, but the messages are still intimate.

Radio-messages are trying to link gaps in communication. Sarajevo Radio broadcasts them day and night. Messages are sent from people in Sarajevo to their friends and relatives in other places in Bosnia and abroad, and to the people in Sarajevo from the rest of the world.

Packages, if you are well connected, travel with help of UNPROFOR, Caritas, Adra, Red Cross, Dobrotvor. Their journey lasts between forty-five to eighty days. Their content is conditioned by the fierce rules of the aggressor. The weight cannot be over 24 kilos, it can't contain meat, vegetables, cans. It happens sometimes that instead of the expected package with food, one receives a piece of a uniform, or stones. More valuable packages don't reach their destination.

Telephone lines

Telephone lines are going through satellites since August of 1992. Those expensive phones — each about $ 50,000 — are with foreign correspondents in the Holiday Inn, in the Office of Defense, in the Police Ministry, and in two industrial strongholds. Since December, citizens could try to get on a waiting list at the Post Office. Waiting is about a week long, and payment is in US dollars, 15-20 per minute, three minutes maximum. Some foreign journalists were known for charging 'their' communication favors i.e. use of satellite telephone, for double the price. That only shows you how expensive it is to go out into the world.

However, it has been observed that lines with that world are working when the Postal tower on the occupied mountain of Trebevic sends a red light. Pay attention, in case you have a working telephone, and a view of the tower! Telephones are also working while the news from Belgrade is on, and while reporters from Pale, from the TV channel called S(erbia in Bosnia), are linking into the Big System. Lines are open during their reports. What you need, again, are a working telephone and quick reflexes.

City communication is reduced to yelling under and in front of large blocks. Where there is no electricity, there can be no bells! Messages are delivered through messengers who carry them from one part of the town to another.

Post offices are not selling Bosnian stamps yet. They haven't been printed. To tell the truth, they aren't necessary. There are no letters that can be mailed.

It is only those scarce taxi-drivers who can establish links between sealed parts of the town. It happens this way: a cab-driver in one zone calls by the car radio his colleague in Grbavica. Then the colleague goes to the address of the person who is being looked for. He tells her to come in the car. While they are driving, conversation goes on. The only disadvantage is that everyone in any cab can eavesdrop.

UNPROFOR, or for those who don't know them: United Nations Protection Forces, were awaited as saviors when they first arrived in Bosnia and Herzegovina with their white vehicles and blue berets. As time went on, they proved to be powerless. Now they are helping in repairs of the infrastructure, in cleaning the city. They are also establishing bureaucratic rules of their own. In some instances proven to be good merchants, they are driving around in trucks, jeeps, transporters. Children are climbing onto their vehicles, and soldiers are throwing them sweets. They transport wounded, bring humanitarian aid, drive from and to the airport. In short, nothing is done without them.

UNPROFOR Headquarters is in the building of Communication Engineering at Alipasino polje. Soldiers are in the barracks which were formerly inhabited by the soldiers of the Yugoslav Peoples Army. The main Headquarters of the UNPROFOR's commander is in a private villa. All these successions seem to be very natural.

Philanthropic organizations are Merhamet, Caritas, Dobrotvor, Adra. Support to its members and sympathizers gives too the Croatian philanthropic organization called Napredak. Although some of these organizations help their members first, and although some of them are based on religious affiliation, Merhamet — Muslim, Caritas — catholic, Dobrotvor — Serbian Orthodox, they are open for the members of other groups. Many are on all lists, in this poverty. Caritas and Adra even bring letters to home addresses. The Jewish community, Jevrejska opstina, established the War Kitchen, which is open to all.

Philantropic organizations

Haircuts are available in some places, within shortened working hours. Everybody wears a coat, there are no lines. It is mostly soldiers who come. Some want to have their head shaved so that a lily is drawn on the skull. A haircut and dying are worth 30 DM. Just so you'll know — salary of those who still work and have something to do is between 10 and 30 DM. By the way, former jobs are now called work obligations.

Haircuts

Watch-repairmen are working, as are the opticians. Locksmiths, electricians, plumbers, carpenters — they will visit your home, if only you can find them. Be ready to pay in hard currency.

Watch repairman

Photographs

Photographs are being made only in the shop next to the Partizan movie-house. They are ready in 24 hours. When there is no electricity, the photographer is making bad polaroids. When there is no electricity and when matters are urgent — photographers from Oslobodjenje will help.

Photocopying: only two places. In the Svjetlost bookstore, or in the Presidency building. The latter choice functions all the time but has one disadvantage. You need to know the right man.

Medical care: its main characteristic is very friendly personnel, which was not the case before the war. It is very efficient. Aside from the hospital and emergency rooms, you will hear quickly about all the improvised ambulances. The maternity hospital has been shelled and is out of use, so babies are born in the regular hospital. When visiting the dentist, you should take your bottle with water, and gloves, which she can use while treating you.

Pharmacies are working, but medicine is mostly missing. Bring your own vitamins. In emergency — look for the locations of Benevolencija and Caritas.

Veterinarian's Clinic

The Veterinarian's Clinic is on Daniel Ozmo Street, in the store where they used to sell hi-fi equipment. Its hours are from 9 a.m. and 2 p.m. Lines are very long, and the service is full, including very complex surgical operations. Sarajevo became the city of abandoned pedigree dogs who are sadly roaming the streets, frozen, hungry and wounded. Their owners have left Sarajevo and left them behind, or they don't have food to even feed themselves.

Sarajevans nowadays go for picnics to Bistrik, Pionirska dolina, or to visit the pipes nearby the Radio and Television Building — all in order to find and get some water. Departure is usually around 6 o'clock in the morning, and the outfit is hiker-style. The picnic lasts approximately five to six hours: some on route, walking, some in line, waiting.

Picnics

demand quite a bit of courage. The best known journalists' routes lead to the front lines: Zlatište — the south-east slope of Trebević, old Sephardic Jewish cemetery destroyed by Serbian trenches, Kobilja glava — north exit from the city, Zuč — a hill which dominates the north side of the city-limits, Vrbanja bridge on which the first casualty of the war fell on April 5, 1992, a young student named Suada Dilberović, Hrasno — a modern part of the city with burned high-rises and numerous grenades falling from the hills all the time. Sarajevans once loved their hills and the fact that city was like a bird in a green nest. In the war, these hills are the sites where the death of Sarajevo is being engineered and spread around, daily.

As an exchange for foreign currency, or for food and drinks, you can find a guide who will take you to all these places, and more: to Dobrinja, the new part of the city which was built for the 1984 Winter Olympics and is now divided by trenches, many of its buildings burned, with cemeteries between the blocks, on the former playgrounds, to Stup, an old neighborhood on the road to West, with the old Catholic church which burned to the ground, to Otes, a medieval village which became the part of the town, with almost 10,000 inhabitants, and which does not exist since the beginning of December of 1992. You can also visit Igman, a mountain once known for its beautiful terrains where you could meet does and wildcats, or go to Stojčevac, the residential complex of Josip Broz Tito — where the first casino opened for the 1984 Winter Olympics. From some of these sites you can get coffee, alcohol, meat and vegetables for a price which is much lower than on the black market. The combination of this mercantile enterprise might lower significantly the price of your tour, and the amount of your fear.

Tours from the city cannot be organized to Jahorina (former famous ski-resort, now the military base of the aggressor), to Trebević (former sledding route, now a front line), to Pale (air-spa, swimming pool, bowling — now the military-political capital of the enemy), to Borike (horseback riding, now cut off from information), Treskavica (hunting and fishing, now a front line), Ilidža (thermal spa, now occupied, ethnically-cleansed territory with a military base).

For the people of Sarajevo, each time they leave their home is a major outing. To visit a friend is an event. Paths lead through back doors, over fences, through gardens, far from the dangerous roads. Visits usually end by staying overnight, for life ends in the early afternoon. In fact, the war-parties are the best kind of entertainment. Once they start, they last until the morning. Hosts are those who, for that evening, have either the electricity, or the drinks.

Cemeteries

The beauty of old Sarajevo cemeteries has been ruined by growing needs. They have been reopened when two contemporary cemeteries — Bare and Vlakovo — became inaccessible. Small old cemeteries which were active for certain neighborhoods, even streets (mahalska) were closed in 1878, with the arrival of the Austro-Hungarian Empire. More than a century later, they started functioning again. People are being buried next to the mosques, on playgrounds in front of their houses. The old military cemeteries — Austrian, of the First Yugoslavia, German, and a partisan one — are full. Since September, the small stadium in the sports complex Koševo, was turned into a cemetery, too. Funerals are held in early morning or dusk hours, to avoid the shelling. There is a rule not to go to the funerals and not to have flowers and wreaths. They cannot be bought anyway, even if someone would want to.

Going out of town

Officially, there is no such thing as 'going out of town'. Since April of 1992, the City has been forced to turn into itself and to greet those who come fulfilling their diplomatic, journalistic and humanitarian tasks.

Convoy

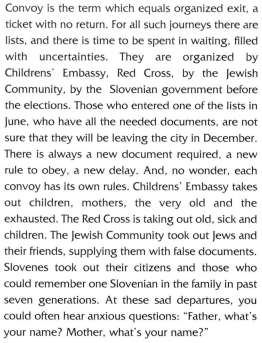

Convoy is the term which equals organized exit, a ticket with no return. For all such journeys there are lists, and there is time to be spent in waiting, filled with uncertainties. They are organized by Childrens' Embassy, Red Cross, by the Jewish Community, by the Slovenian government before the elections. Those who entered one of the lists in June, who have all the needed documents, are not sure that they will be leaving the city in December. There is always a new document required, a new rule to obey, a new delay. And, no wonder, each convoy has its own rules. Childrens' Embassy takes out children, mothers, the very old and the exhausted. The Red Cross is taking out old, sick and children. The Jewish Community took out Jews and their friends, supplying them with false documents. Slovenes took out their citizens and those who could remember one Slovenian in the family in past seven generations. At these sad departures, you could often hear anxious questions: "Father, what's your name? Mother, what's your name?"

One more paradigmatic dialogue:

Question: "When are you leaving?"

Answer: "Well, I am on the list. Still waiting for a confirmation from Geneva."

Discreetly, but to no one's surprise, the City was left by wives, children, parents and friends of various officials. Illegal channels were used, starting in Stup, Ilidža, Kobiljač a. From there, to Kiseljak — a Hong Kong of Sarajevo — if heading West. To Pale, if going East. On each of these starts, there was a 'connection', a guy dealing with the formalities which basically means exchanging tangible hard currency with the invisible bus ticket. Starting fee is 100 to 200 DM. Additional amounts were supplied by Muslims, for they often needed false documents.

It is a well known secret that for about 1000 DM, deposited in one of the cafes close to the Veterinary college, one could get to Grbavica (a sealed part of the town, a camp from which no one can go out, and into which no one can enter). From there, for the mentioned fee, the bus would take you to Belgrade. Another part of the same secret is that there is a rule according to which for one person who enters Grbavica, one from Grbavica is being released into the City. Profit is mutual.

Airport runway

Crossing the airport runway...It is necessary to cross the barricade which blocks the neighborhood of Dobrinja. You need a dark night. Wounded, or those who look like that, are taken by car. The control procedure of the Blue Helmets is very kind. With a financial agreement, one can pass in the first try. The airport runway is the only city promenade. True, in one night, the Blue Helmets may return no less than 260 people, but one can do it somehow. The attempt to run costs between 100 and 200 DM. Still, there are some tips to be remembered. The runway is equipped with photo-cells and sensors which detect anyone who might be walking by. This trap, installed by UNPROFOR, may surprise you with alarms or spotlights which go on immediately after you are spotted. Different divisions of the UN force — the Blue Helmets — react in accordance with their national, regional and personal sense of humor. The French are amused by our wit. Ukrainians are made nervous by our stubbornness, but they can be talked into a deal. The best guys are the Egyptians. They are running after the old lady who is smuggling a carton of bananas from Hrasnica to Dobrinja. They forgive the guy who is running with crutches. One such guy was forced to return no less then eight times; the ninth time he wrote his own obituary in French. Since the French have respect for the dead, he left the city on the air-transport. All sides catch smugglers, but also those who manage to crawl across half the runway. In short, the journey is hard, but once the basics are completed, and you are on the right side, everything is a matter of superstructure —skill, papers, money. It is no secret that for 1000 to 2000 DM one can fly out on a humanitarian aid plane. The only drawback is that there are no guarantees at which airport you are going to land.

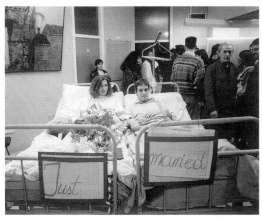

Tourism in Sarajevo comes down to foreign journalists and politicians. The latter ones stay in the city only for a few hours and run away. Soldiers and journalists stay longer, but are regularly replaced. Only for the people of Sarajevo is there no exit. They don't live in shifts. Journalists are either in the Holiday Inn, or with friends who have a good basement. They travel the city in protected cars, and with obligatory bullet-proof vests.

Sarajevo has numerous hotels. They are all full, except for the Bristol and Posta. They became homes for refugees. The same goes for the oldest and the most famous hotel, Evropa, in the part which has not burned. With war, the Evropa was completely emptied — of its kitchen, silverware, crystal glasses, tablecloths, paintings, furniture. Food and drinks are gone since April, too.

Guests are accepted only in the HOLIDAY INN, a hotel with two directors. One was appointed by the City Parliament, the other one by the Republic. Of course, not all of the rooms are available, for some no longer exist. During stronger shelling, guests leave their rooms and sleep collectively in the basement, armed with their cellular phones. The hotel is well supplied with alcoholic drinks and refreshments. Only there can you try the best of local couisine — big selections of Viennese and Oriental delights.

Guests are, of course, foreign journalists. There are some locals, too. These are private businessmen, merchants, people for all times and all imaginable businesses. Prices are war-like. The average menu is 50 DM per person. If ready for the black market rates, you may try to pay in the local currency. Service is decent.

At night, the hotel resembles Casablanca.

Culinary specialties are offered, since last October, in the following places:

GURMAN (Gourmet). Location: Corner of Titova and Radojke Lakić Street.

BUJRUM (Welcome). Location: Above the Cathedral, in the Vuk Karadžic Street.

KRALJICA DUNAVA (Queen of Danube). Location: Kata Govorušić Street.

KLUB NOVINARA (Journalist's Club). Location: Pavle Goranin Street.

The selection of drinks is very limited. As for the food—aside from soup one can get cooked veal, hamburgers (domestic version is called pljeskavica). How the food actually gets there is kept as the biggest professional secret. Silent are both those who order and those who deliver. And those who eat.

There are private clubs, too. In case you have someone to take you there, look for:
MONIK (behind the Post office at Dolac Malta)
MAZESTIK (close to Jugobanka)
RAGUZA (next to the main market — Markale)
JEZ (neighborhood of the seat of the Yugoslav People's Army)

Modern, prewar life of cafes, in which mingled the youth of the city, and its business circles...Good music, excellent coffee, whiskey, home-made brandy. Since November they re-emerged, protected with thick slabs and UNHCR foils, with generators for their own electricity. Their names: Bugatti, Piere, Stefanel, Charlie, Sky, Indi, Holland, 501, S.O.S., GoGo, Tvin...They start working at 11 a.m. and close at nightfall. Some work until the curfew — visit only if you have a friend who knows the city well. Some are open as long as there are guests. All are armed.

There are places where you can gamble, playing cards. It is convenient for foreigners —payment is in hard currency anyway. One shouldn't have too much self-confidence. Sarajevo gamblers cannot reach Italy or Cote de Azur any more. Their skilled passion has to be fulfilled here.

Coffee shops
Sarajevo had its first coffee-shop more than four hundred years ago. They spread quickly, hundreds of them, and became very popular places for gathering and slow enjoyment. Their offering was limited, but what was offered was of the best quality: Turkish coffee (Bosnian version), tea and fir-tree juice. As time went by, European-style cafes merged with those where the cold, sour-sweet yellowish nature melted in water, and black, warm substance were the only tastes, and dzezva, fildzan and rahatlokum were the only objects. They introduced espresso, pastry, and alcohol. Both styles lived together, beloved and nurtured by the same public.

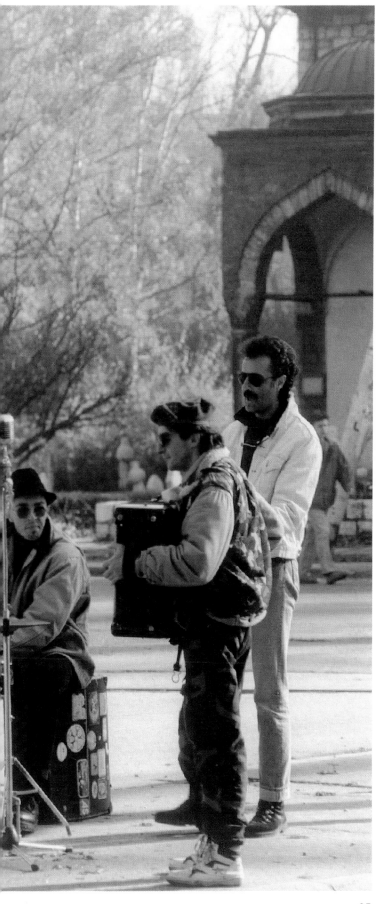

Once a week in the partially destroyed Red Cross building in the "Sniper Alley". Exhibitions by the local sculptors, painters and "conceptualists". Hot tea is also served. The gallery owned by "Scena obala".

"Kamerni teatar 55" is located in a shelled building in the main street, Marshal Tito 55. The auditorium is one of the safest places in the city. Every day at 1 p.m. (the time is determined by the difficulty of moving about in the lightless city at night) there is a performance, a presentation of a new bank, newspaper, or a commemoration of some significant event...

Sometimes there are cocktail-parties where the humanitarian aid is served. *Hair* is the most popular hit.

"Scena obala". Once a week at 1 p.m. The place is safe. The auditorium sits 100 people. Heating by battery. Movies are on video tapes. The cinema is also a meeting place for intellectuals, foreign newsmen and artists.

Those with batteries/generators can listen to the government radio and some independent, privately owned stations. The most popular are the urban stations "Zid" and "Studio 99"

The daily OSLOBODJENJE which is published in a completely destroyed building. When there is no sufficient paper it is published in small edition and the news vendors stick the sheets onto the facades. Also available are RATNI DANI and BLIC, the magazine TENNIS, the magazine of the Architects' Association.
Travelers also bring into the city old issues of the dailies and weeklies from the former Yugoslavia and elsewhere. These papers circulate from house to house.

Cinema

Radio

Newspapers

Cultural survival

The beseiged city defends itself by culture and thus survives. Groups and individuales create whatever they used to create before the siege. In impossible circumstances they produce films, write books, publish newspapers, produce radio programs, design postcards, stage exhibitions, performances, make blueprints for rebuilding the city, found new banks, organize fashion shows, shoot photographs, celebrate holidays, put on make up...

Sarajevo is the city of the future and of the life in the post-cataclysm. In it on the ruins of the old civilization a new one is sprouting, an alternative one, composed of remains of urban elements. Sarajevo lives a life of futuristic comics and science fiction movies.

Tips

When you come to Sarajevo, be prepared and be mature. It might prove to be the most important decision you have ever made in your life. Bring: good shoes which make you walk long and run fast, pants with many pockets, pills for water, Deutsche Marks (small denomination), batteries, matches, jar with vitamins, canned food, drinks and cigarettes. Everything you bring will be consumed or exchanged for useful information. You should know when to skip a meal, how to turn trouble into a joke and be relaxed in impossible moments. Learn not to show emotions and don't be fussy about anything. Be ready to sleep in basements, eager to walk and work surrounded by danger. Give up all your former habits. Use the telephone when it works, laugh when it doesn't. You'll laugh a lot. Despise, don't hate.

If you play with lines on the map of Europe, you will have to find Sarajevo. It is revealed where lines cross over the Balkans. First you draw a line from Paris, through Venice and then to Istanbul, the closest East that Europe knew for centuries. A second line starts in Northern Europe, goes between Berlin and Warsaw, through the Mediterranean, and then to Africa. These lines meet over Bosnia and Herzegovina. And, in fact, they cross over Sarajevo.

Here wars were started and here they went on, while people loved and longed for love. Here merchants were selling goods from all over the world and life was close and distant to ways of the East and the West. It was Western for the East, and Oriental for the West. It was the life of Sarajevo.

History

Its poet, Muhamed Nerkesi (1592-1634), far from his beloved city, wrote:"Nothing comes close to my city. It is the pearl on the earth, saraj of springs and gardens,unique in the world...High mountains around it, old and noble, snow-peaks covered with mist are kissing the sky...It is impossible, no doubt, to name all the beauties of this place..."